D1303335

Look What Came From the Netherlands

by
Kevin Davis

Franklin Watts
A Division of Scholastic Inc.
New York Toronto London Auckland Sydney
Mexico City New Delhi Hong Kong
Danbury, Connecticut

Series Concept: Shari Joffe
Design: Steve Marton

Library of Congress Cataloging-in-Publication Data

Davis, Kevin.
   Look What Came From the Netherlands / by Kevin Davis.
      p. cm. — (Look what came from series)
   Includes bibliographical references and index.
   Summary: Describes many things that originally came from the
Netherlands, including inventions, fashion, customs and holidays,
sports, food, animals, and words.
      ISBN 0-531-11961-0 (lib. bdg.)   0-531-16631-7 (pbk.)
      1. Netherlands—Civilization—Juvenile literature.
2. Civilization—Dutch influences—Juvenile literature.   I. Title.
II. Series.
      DJ71 .D344 2002
      949.2—dc21   2002005299

Photographs © 2002: Archive Photos/Getty Images: 8, 17 bottom right (Hulton Getty Collection); Art Resource, NY: 3; b en u International Picture Service: 19 top; Bata Shoe Museum, Toronto: 16 top; Corbis Images: 20 right, 21 left (Dave Bartruff), 16 bottom, 23 (Owen Franken), 15 bottom right, 15 top right (Kit Houghton); Envision: 18 right, 19 left (Kenneth Chen), 20 left (Mark Ferri), cover top right, 18 top (Steven Needham); Hollandse Hoogte: 21 (Jurjen Drenth), 19 bottom (Ton Poortvliet); Mary Evans Picture Library: 9 bottom; Nance S. Trueworthy: 26 right, 26 left, 27 left, 27 top right, 27 bottom right; North Wind Picture Archives: cover bottom right, 11 right, 15 left, 24 left, 25 right; Philips Electronics: 13 bottom; Photo Researchers, NY: 6 left (Dr. Jeremy Burgess/SPL), 7 left (D.A. Calvert/Royal Greenwich Observatory/SPL), 4 (Christian Grzimek/Okapia), 14 (James King-Holmes), 17 top (Robin Laurance), 7 right (SPL); Photodisc, Inc.: 1 left, 1 right, 24 bottom right, 25 left; Rigoberto Quinteros: 13 top left, 13 top right; Science Museum/Science & Society Picture Library: 12; Stock Boston/ Jon Feingersh: 9 top; Stock Montage, Inc.: 11 left, 22; Stone/Getty Images: borders (D.J. Ball), 24 top right (Dave Nagel), 10 (Charles Thatcher); The Image Works: 32 left (Tony Arruza), cover bottom left (Sonda Dawes); Viesti Collection, Inc.: 17 bottom left (Lee), cover background (Bill Terry); Visuals Unlimited/Henry Aldrich: 6 right.

Contents

Greetings from the Netherlands!

The flag
of the
Netherlands

The Netherlands is a small and beautiful country in western Europe. It is also known as Holland. The people of the Netherlands are called Dutch.

When people think of this country, they often picture a land of windmills, tulips, and wooden shoes. But this fascinating place has contributed many great things to the world, from telescopes to doughnuts!

The Netherlands is a low-lying country. That means much of the land is at or below sea level. At one time, more than two-fifths of the country was underwater! The Dutch people dug canals and built walls called dikes to prevent cities and towns from getting flooded.

The Netherlands was once home to many great explorers who sailed around the world in search of new lands and people. So let's explore this interesting place and see what came from the Netherlands!

Inventions

Replica of Leeuwenhoek's precision microscope

Antonie van Leeuwenhoek

A very important invention from the Netherlands helped people see very tiny things. Around 1590, a Dutch eyeglass maker named Zacharias Jansen put two lenses on opposite ends of a tube. He used this device to look at tiny objects. It was called a **compound microscope.**

Another Dutch inventor, Antonie van Leeuwenhoek, was the first to make a high-powered **precision microscope.** This allowed a person to see even smaller things. It used one tiny lens but could magnify things much larger and more clearly than the compound microscope. It allowed people to see bacteria, which had not been seen before.

Galileo's 1609 telescope was based on Lipperschey's design.

Microscopes are great for looking at tiny things. Another Dutch invention helped people see large things that are very far away. Hans Lipperschey invented the first **telescope** about 400 years ago. It was called a *kijker,* which meant "looker." The famous Italian astronomer Galileo later made his own telescopes for looking at stars and planets.

Dredger from the 1700s

Because the Netherlands was often flooded, people who lived there dug canals to carry away water and prevent flooding. About 400 years ago, the Dutch invented a machine called a **dredger** to clear mud and weeds from waterways. The dredger also was used to help make dams.

Many people came up with the idea of a **submarine**. One of the first to succeed in making one was Cornelis Drebbel, a Dutchman who lived nearly 400 years ago. His submarine was a funny-looking thing. It was made of greased leather stretched over a wooden frame. It had oars that came out of the sides through waterproof flaps. The first submarine went only about 15 feet (4.6 meters) underwater.

Many homes have a device on the wall that controls the temperature inside. This amazing invention, called a **thermostat**, was also invented by Drebbel. A modern thermostat "knows" when a room gets above or below a certain temperature, and then turns on or off a furnace or air conditioner to keep the room comfortable.

Modern-day thermostat

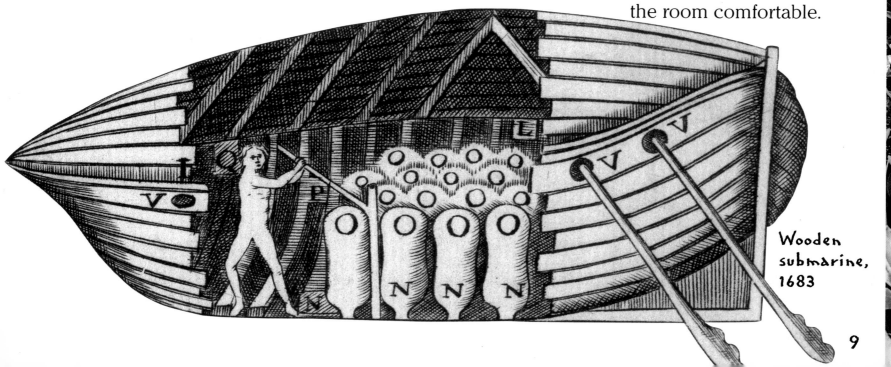

Wooden submarine, 1683

9

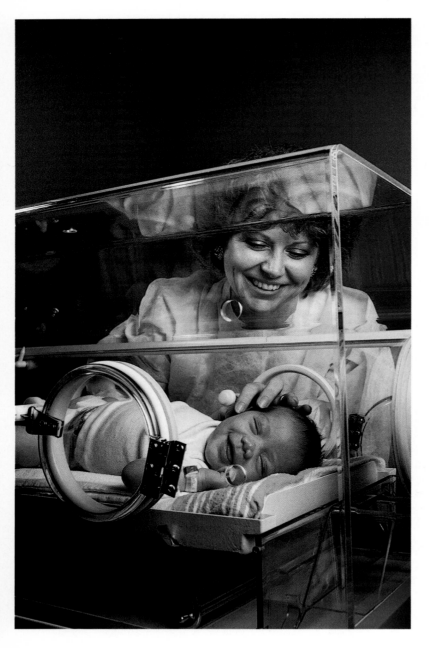

Drebbel used his idea for the thermostat to invent the **incubator.** The first incubator was used to keep chicken eggs warm so they would hatch even without a mother bird sitting on them. Today, modern incubators have many uses. Schools and zoos use them so children can watch chicks hatch. Hospitals use incubators to keep newborn babies warm when they are very small and sick.

Modern-day incubator

Huygens presenting his pendulum clock to King Louis XIV of France

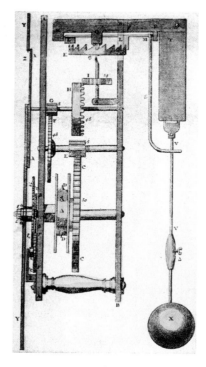

The pendulum mechanism of Huygen's clock

A pendulum is a weight that swings back and forth. About 350 years ago, Dutch inventor Christiaan Huygens added a pendulum to a clock to help the clock keep better time. The regular swing of the pendulum helped keep the clock accurate to within five minutes a day. Before the invention of this **pendulum clock,** clocks could gain or lose a whole hour every day!

more inventions

An early
pocket watch

Huygens also made another great timekeeping invention—the **pocket watch.** The portable clock had been invented in Germany, but Huygens added a spring and balance wheel to make it more reliable.

Have you ever used an **audiocassette tape recorder?** The Philips Electronics Company made the first one in the Netherlands in 1963. The company allowed other companies to use their design, and now cassettes are used all over the world.

Audiocassette tape

Modern-day audiocassette tape recorder

The first audiocassette tape recorder

Holstein Friesian cow

Animals

If you drink milk, chances are pretty good that it came from a cow whose ancestors came from the Netherlands. The **Holstein Friesian** cow is one of the most popular dairy cows in the world. This kind of cow is usually very large and has black and white spots.

A horse called the **Friesian** came from the Netherlands thousands of years ago. It was very popular in the Middle Ages because it was good in battle. In the 1600s, it was used as a riding horse. Later, people used this type of horse for pulling wagons or small carriages that carried one or two people.

Another horse, the **Dutch draught horse,** also came from the Netherlands. This big, powerful work horse was first bred about 100 years ago. It is known to be smart and hardworking.

Dutch draught horse

Friesian horses being used in battle in the Middle Ages

Modern-day Friesian horse

15

Dutch wooden clog from the 1400s

Fashion

Modern-day Dutch clogs

People in the Netherlands are believed to have been among the first to wear wooden shoes hundreds of years ago. These shoes are also known as **clogs.** The Dutch call them *klompen.*

People in the Netherlands wore wooden shoes to protect their feet against the wet, soggy land. The shoes were made in many different colors, depending on the region.

Dutch people generally don't wear their wooden shoes indoors. It's the custom to leave them outside.

16

Clog maker in Amsterdam

Women in the Netherlands also used to wear a beautiful type of hat made with lace called a **Volendam cap.** It was named after a fishing village. This traditional cap fits close to the head. Dancers in Volendam wore these hats as part of their costumes.

The Dutch usually leave their wooden shoes outside.

Dutch girls wearing Volendam caps

Food

Can you imagine eating a doughnut without a hole in the middle? Well, that's how the first **doughnut** looked when it was made in the Netherlands in the 1500s. The idea for the hole came from the United States about 200 years later.

In the Netherlands, the doughnut was a deep-fried pastry called *olykoek,* or "oil cake." It was made of sweet dough and had sugar sprinkled on top. Dutch people brought recipes for this treat when they came to the United States in the 1600s. Because each pastry was the size of a walnut, people called them "doughnuts."

No one knows for sure who invented the doughnut with a hole. A popular story is that it was an old sea captain. His mother made doughnuts for him, but he thought they were too mushy. The captain poked holes in the dough so it would not be so gooey in the middle and would cook better. It worked! The idea caught on, and people started making doughnuts with holes in them.

Today, people in the Netherlands still enjoy little ball-shaped doughnuts called *oliebollen.*

The first doughnuts probably looked similar to these.

Oliebollen being served on
New Year's Eve

Dutch women making oliebollen

These delicious raisin-filled pastries are
traditionally served on New Year's Eve.

more food

Edam cheese

cruller

Gouda cheese

Another popular pastry, the **cruller,** also came from the Netherlands. It is a long, twisted, doughnut-like pastry with a sweet coating. The word "cruller" comes from the Dutch word *krullen,* which means "curl."

Two delicious cheeses—**Gouda** and **Edam**—are named after small towns in the Netherlands. Both are mild, yellow cheeses. They usually have a red or yellow wax covering.

Cheese market in the town of Gouda

Customs

Christmas wouldn't be the same without jolly old **Santa Claus.** But did you know the idea for Santa came from the Netherlands?

Long ago, the Dutch began celebrating a special holiday on December 6 honoring St. Nicholas. This holiday is called Sinterklaas Day. It had no relation to Christmas. Dutch people of all religions celebrated this holiday.

St. Nicholas was a Catholic bishop known for giving gifts to the poor. He is the patron saint of children and sailors. On the night before Sinterklaas Day, children received presents and had big meals at home with their families.

Vive St. Nicolas!

Old postcard showing St. Nicholas delivering Christmas gifts

Men dressed in red-and-white bishops' robes to look like St. Nicholas. They went from house to house to ask children if they said their prayers and did their homework. If the children said yes, they got presents.

When Dutch people came to the United States, they brought this tradition with them. American children pronounced *Sinterklaas* as "Santa Claus," and the name stuck. Eventually, Santa Claus became part of the Christmas tradition.

Sinterklaas parade in Amsterdam

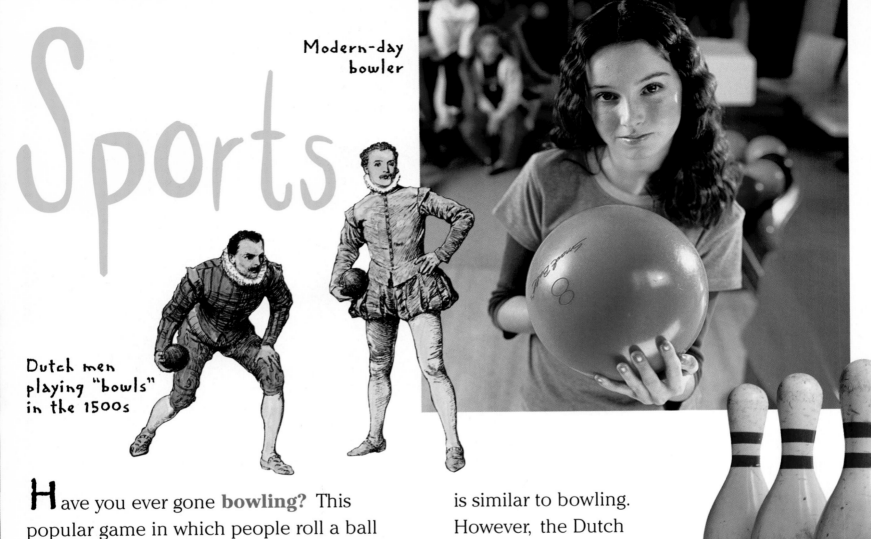

Modern-day bowler

Sports

Dutch men playing "bowls" in the 1500s

Have you ever gone **bowling?** This popular game in which people roll a ball to knock over pins was developed in the Netherlands.

It's true that people in ancient Egypt played a game with pieces of stone and a ball that is similar to bowling. However, the Dutch invented a game that used wooden pins and more closely resembles modern bowling. In the game of Dutch pins,

24

players used nine wooden pins and tried to knock them over with a ball. When Dutch people came to New York, they brought the game with them. It became modern bowling and now uses ten pins.

In the 1600s, the Dutch brought bowling to North America.

Modern-day bowling pins

Making paper tulips

Tulips originally came from Turkey, but in the 1600s, the Netherlands became one of the most important places in the world for growing and selling tulips. Today, the Netherlands is still famous for its tulips. You can make your own paper tulips with a few simple items.

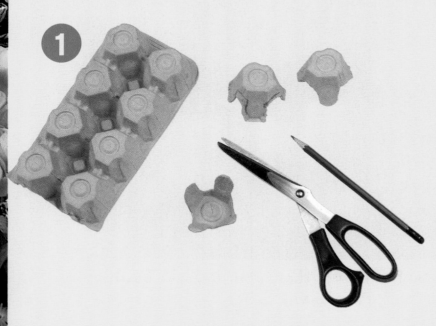

You'll need the following materials:
- Colored plastic or Styrofoam egg carton
- Scissors   · Pencil   · Glue
- Ruler   · Yellow or orange yarn
- Three 7-inch pieces of stiff wire
- Green construction paper
- Green floral tape

1. Cut the egg carton into single cups. Draw four petal shapes around the outside of each cup. Cut around the lines to make tulip shapes.

2. Draw outlines of four leaves on construction paper and cut them out. Brush glue on one side of each leaf. Place a 7-inch (18-centimeter) piece of wire in the center of a leaf, leaving about 3 inches (8 cm) of wire on the bottom.

Put another leaf cutout on the other side of the wire to match up with the first leaf and press them together. Do the same with another set of leaves on a second piece of wire. Wrap the pieces of wire with floral tape, starting at the bottom of each leaf.

3. Cut yarn into four 2-inch (5-cm) pieces. These will be the flower stamens. Take another piece of wire, about 8 inches (20 cm) long, and bend the end of it over to form an open loop. Place the yarn pieces inside the loop and twist the loop tightly to hold the yarn. This will be the stem of the flower.

4. Ask an adult to use the scissors to punch a small hole in the bottom of the tulip cup. Insert the wire with the stamens into the cup and pull it through until the stamens rest at the bottom of the tulip. You can use glue at the bottom of the tulip to help hold the stamens in place. Wrap the wire under the tulip cup several times with floral tape.

5. Place the leaf wires on each side of the stem. Wrap tape around all three wires to the end of the stem so it holds the leaves on tightly.

27

How do you say...?

Dutch and English came from the same family of languages. As you can see, some Dutch words are similar to English words.

English	Dutch	How to pronounce it
hello	hallo	hal-LOH
goodbye	tot ziens	TOTE-zeans
please	alstublieft	ahl-stew-BLEEFT
thank you	dank u	DAHNK-uuh
cheese	kaas	kahs
clock	klok	klawk
cow	koe	coo
house	paard	part
shoe	schoen	skhoon
tulip	tulp	tulp

To find out more

Here are some other resources to help you learn more about the Netherlands:

Books

Geography Department.
Netherlands in Pictures
(Visual Geography Series).
Lerner Publications, 1992.

Hintz, Martin. **The Netherlands**
(Enchantment of the World, 2nd
Series). Children's Press, 1999.

Seth, Ronald. **The Netherlands**
(Major World Nations).
Chelsea House Publishers, 1997.

Seward, Pat. **Netherlands**
(Cultures of the World). Benchmark
Books, 1995.

Organizations and Online Sites

The Flying Dutchman's Page
http://www.proqc.com/~jeroen/
main.html
Facts about the country, history,
links to news, magazines, sports
information, and a virtual tour
through the Netherlands.

The Holland Ring
http://www.thehollandring.com/
index.html
A very big web site with Dutch
history, folklore and culture, links
to museums, historical sites, Dutch
cooking sites, and home pages of
Dutch people.

Visit Holland
http://www.visitholland.com
This site includes tourist information,
facts about the country, and activities
from the Netherlands Board of Tourism.

Glossary

accurate to be correct or exact

ancestors relatives who lived long ago

astronomer person who studies the heavenly bodies

bacteria very tiny living things

bishop high-ranking leader of the church

breed to reproduce animals that have certain qualities

custom the usual way of doing things

dam barrier to hold back a flow of water

Europe continent located between Asia and the Atlantic Ocean

lens round piece of glass that makes things look bigger or helps people see better

Middle Ages period of history in Europe from A.D. 476-1450

modern occurring at the present time

precision very detailed, accurate

reliable able to depend on

resembles looks like

tradition activity, event, or custom that has been handed down from generation to generation

Index

Look what doesn't come from the Netherlands!

Even though the Netherlands is known as the land of **windmills,** they were actually invented in ancient Persia. They were first used to grind grain and did not look like windmills today. The sails were horizontal rather than vertical.

Meet the Author

Kevin Davis loves to travel and write about the interesting places he has visited. He is a journalist and author who lives in Chicago. This book is dedicated to Adam and Dorie Fox and their wonderful family.